Pandorama

Ian Duhig worked with homeless people for
fifteen years before devoting himself to writing
activities full-time. He has won the Forward Best Poem
Prize once and the National Poetry Competition twice.
His last two books with Picador, *The Lammas Hireling*
(2003) and *The Speed of Dark* (2007), were both PBS
Choices and shortlisted for the T. S. Eliot Prize. His
most recent short story appeared in *The New Uncanny*,
winner of the Shirley Jackson Best Anthology Award
for 2008, and his most recent musical collaboration,
with the Clerks early music consort, on their CD
Don't Talk – Just Listen (Signum, 2009). He lives
in Leeds with his wife Jane and their son Owen.

Also by Ian Duhig

The Bradford Count

The Mersey Goldfish

Nominies

The Lammas Hireling

The Speed of Dark

Ian Duhig

Pandorama

PICADOR

First published 2010 by Picador
an imprint of Pan Macmillan, a division of Macmillan Publishers Limited
Pan Macmillan, 20 New Wharf Road, London N1 9RR
Basingstoke and Oxford
Associated companies throughout the world
www.panmacmillan.com

ISBN 978-0-330-52124-6

9 8 7 6 5 4 3 2 1

A CIP catalogue record for this book is available from
the British Library.

Printed in the UK by CPI Mackays, Chatham ME5 8TD

Contents

goths

I love them. They bring a little antilife and uncolour
to the Corn Exchange on city centre shopping days,
as if they had all just crawled out of that *Ringu* well,
so many Sadakos dripping tarnished silver jewellery
onto the undead fashions they dig up in fleamarkets.
They are the black that is always the new black.
Their perfume lingers, freshly-turned-grave sweet.

Black sheep, they pilgrimage twice a year to Whitby,
through our landscape of dissolved monastery and pit,
toasting themselves in cider'n'blackcurrant, vegan blood.
They dance macabre at gigs like the Dracula Spectacula.
The next morning, lovebitten and wincing in the sunlight,
they take photos of each other, hoping they won't develop.

Boxeur Nègre

Now it's that Matisse papier découpé
summoned by this glimpsed silhouette;
once it was my brother shadow-boxing,
circling the square ring with Dick Tiger.

Roll, block, draw, jab as Joey Giardello
in Atlantic City slipped Tiger's crosses,
harder body shots, that worse left hook,
always eluding Tiger like the real money.

Rough Music

I heard this from a Cleator man,
 ex-miner, hard as nails,
whose folks were Famine migrants there,
 though first they'd stopped in Wales –

in Rhymni Ironworks their kind
 got jobs they couldn't keep,
you don't impress Welsh foremen when
 you're always half-asleep;

for locals played their famed 'Rough Music'
 on pipes and drums all night
while marching round the Irish camp
 from dusk till morning light.

They moved to Cleator, soon to hear
 its Orange Lodge now planned
that riot-rousing Murphy'd stir
 their sleepy local band.

Instead the Irish miners marched
 to meet him when he'd come:
they played the pipes with Murphy's tripes
 then beat him like a drum.

This outrage caused that Lodge to grow
 the biggest in the world,
but folk grew sick of stone and stick,
 soon all its banners furled.

So all you migrants heed my call
    to first give peace a chance;
should neighbours then still vex your labours –
    make a song and dance.

Charivari

Derived from *chav*, we call this *charivari* –
rough music from us roughnecks plus a skit.
Our instruments aren't made by Stradivari,
they're anything that we can reach to hit.

The drum to Ambrose meant eternal death,
but that's exactly why we like it most:
enjoy your wealth until your dying breath,
for then you'll spend eternity as toast.

Jerome thought sinful music sounds so good
the pious kind should strike one's ear as raw;
so if we sound less polished than we should,
it's just because we take Jerome as law.

Shaw's Hell was full of amateur musicians –
we're worse than amateur, yet we're up here
to give the lie to art and its beauticians
for one day of the calendar each year.

The music that the Antichrist will play
is beautiful beyond our power to tell,
and Paganini took our breath away
as Lucifer his soul away to Hell.

You've heard that truth is beauty, beauty truth
like one was Castor and the other Pollux –
forgive the language of uncultured youth,
but Cockney Keats was talking Hampstead bollocks.

Because the beautiful can prove untrue,
you sometimes need to heed Tom, Dick and Harry.
We're here to drum that message into you,
and that's the meaning of the charivari.

'Strata' Smith

Mine's a common surname for a born nobody,
a blacksmith's boy from that low stratum where
language beats on your ears and means it.

I learned from navvies, paviours, molecatchers;
miners brought words with their sacks of fossils
which I used: pundib, clunch, coral rag, cornbrash –

a system of names barbarous on ears polite,
wrote a gentleman from the Geological Society,
but I mapped a whole world beneath his feet.

Out of debtors' gaol, I tramped that world again.
Above my grave, they raised a sandstone block
so soft, all the words wore off in bad weather.

Jingwei Birds

A ranger in the old Immigrants' Station on Angel Island
noticed how shadows rippled on some replastered walls;
he found this was done to cover poems carved there
by the Chinese applying to navvy on the railways.

A dragon out of water
is at the mercy of ants;
brats can bait caged tigers
but I will have vengeance . . .

Another in classic style invoked the famous Jingwei bird
that Yandi's daughter became on drowning in the sea,
a sea which in turn the bird tried to drown with pebbles,
flying them from the Western Mountains, one at a time.

Jericho Shanty

*Decent people, them as lives in towns and villages and has
homes of their own and no occasion to tramp, they gets a
notion in their heads as we belong to a different breed . . .
only t'other day I heard a woman telling about a railway
accident, and she said as there were three men killed, and
a navvy* – reported by Reverend Louis Moule Evans

I Jericho Shanty

Named by the navvies themselves from where
they were always being told to go: elsewhere.

II A Different Breed

Legends clung like muck to navvies
with names such as One-Eyed Conro,
Thick-Lipped Blondin, Cat-eating Scan,
Contrary York, Half-Ear Slen, Moleskin Joe
who whipped a parson with his own lap-dog.
Each shifted two pounds of bully beef
and twenty tons of rubble every day;
Godless sectarians, their rhyming language
excommunicated missionaries or spies
and they would riot just for the crack.
They sold wives for ale; to anatomists,
the bodies of comrades whose real names
they never came to know, who wouldn't
have told their next of kin anyway.
What's to say? End of. Amen.

III Ornithology

The beak of his pick
    strikes earthfast stone;
the navvy's cry
    is the pickbird's song.

IV The Miracle of Blea Moor

The Irish and English
    digging together:
on lugs of long spades
    each a left-footer,

the Prod and the Pape
    as brother with brother:
no God could do this,
    only Blea weather.

V Legends

Walker's 'Fragments' were men like Half Dai,
crippled navvies he kept on as watchmen,
missing fingers, toes, arms, legs, senses –
once, a graveyard shift could only muster
a single eye between them like the Graeae,
but they would have paggered any Perseus
then handed him over to the constabulary.

VI Ribblehead Viaduct

acid rain
    owl light
polished plate
    foul bite

under the bridgework,
    teeth of air
navvies whistle
    elsewhere

VII The Work of the Giants

the work of the Giants, the stonesmiths . . .
    . . . by files grim-ground . . .

these many meadhalls men filled
  with loud cheerfulness . . .

    . . . hot springs, loosed,
ran over hoar stone . . . . . .

Earthgrip holds them fast
in gravesgrasp . . .

    . . . shone the old skilled work

    . . . rime on mortar

Chang Cheng

Qin's wall as Englished
renders Chang *Great*,
a gain in translation
its builders don't share;

they'd treat it with humour
in such as this ballad
the Wu Music Bureau
reluctantly gathered:

Though slow rose Qin's Wall,
It was fast his line fell;
We laugh at the fool
As our grandchildren will!

One brick they honour,
now with its own plinth:
in a thousand-li length,
their margin for error.

Unmaking

Boar-hunting spears have a cross-piece to stop
a spitted beast driving up its shaft to the lord,
but in the Ritual of Unmaking it hold his cuts;
heart, liver, sweetmeats steaming like thurifers.

The inside of the boar's skin serves as tablecloth
to feast the lord's hounds on humbles and lights,
while a retained poet, silken in words and livery,
furnishes all his lord's kills lavishly with meanings.

When rubbed the wrong way, their living bristles
stab back. Gorged on mast and fruit in ferment,
they brawl among themselves, can gut a horse.
Tusky tusky, they whisper, which means nothing.

Róisín Bán

The M1 laid, they laid us off;
we stayed where it ran out in Leeds,
a white rose town in love with roads,
its Guinness smooth, its locals rough.

Some nights we'd drink in Chapeltown,
a place not known for Gaeligores,
to hear Ó Catháin sing sean-nós –
Ó Riada gave him the crown.

Though most were lost by 'Róisín Dubh',
all knew his art was rich and strange
in the pub we drowned with our own black stuff
when we laid the Sheepscar Interchange.

Pulped books help asphalt stick to roads
and cuts down traffic-sound as well;
between the lines a navvy reads
black seas of words that did not sell.

Beggar's Song

from Alarcón

Alms, please, be kind;
there is no sadder thing
than to be blind
in a Yorkshire spring.

Via Negativa

Not circumcellion, beggar, gyrovague
but Lagos Christian college boy.
Not abbey-lubber but job-seeker.

Not City of God but Motorway City.
Not office career but casual labour.
Not Union member but *Last In First Out*.

Not My Father's Mansion but Chapeltown slum.
Not *Welcome Brother* but *rent up front*.
Not Empire pilgrim but evicted vagrant.

Not *Ambulare pro Deo* but *Wandering Abroad*.
Not *Ave Maria* but Black Maria.
Not demonic visions but brain damage.

Not Church Latin but medical Latin.
Not Catechism but questionnaires.
Not Pentecost tongues but echolalia.

Not the African Fathers but *the African Mind*.
Not Divine Spark but ECT.
Not Cloud of Unknowing but Largactil fog.

Not confessional boxes but cardboard boxes.
Not the Body of Christ at Holy Communion
but the cold host of a Leeds moon.

Not *via negativa* but fugue state.
Not River of Life but *Rivers of blood*.
Not rosary beads but bubbles of air.

Not fisher of men but fished from a weir.
Not heavenly throne but pauper's grave.
Not heavenly choir but football chant:

And you shouldn't trust a copper
if your name's Oluwale
and you can't find your way home.

Flooding Back

i.m. David Oluwale

In Ovid's *Metamorphoses* Book VIII,
he hangs fresh wreaths on branches of the trees
that Baucis and Philemon had become
at the same moment the old couple died.
To save them from the pain of either's loss,
they'd begged this gift from gods they'd taken in
when every other door was closed on them.
But masked gods walk among us as a test,
for hospitality's a sacred duty
binding all who claim morality;
on their high ground, Baucis and Philemon
were safe in their dilapidated home
when judgement visited the town below,
and neighbours' tears, withheld for homeless gods,
now swelled a tidal wave that rose and fell
on mansion as on hovel, bank as church;
a flood as levelling as that first great flood
when dead fish perched like scaly birds in trees
or wreaths left by respectful votaries,
while underneath, waves billowed like blown wheat
on wheatfields yielding only anchor-holds,
as if the Aire became that element
it sounded always destined to become,
a change to take the breath away from men.

from 'The Masque of Blankness'

The first and most constant problem with the City of Leeds
is to find it. There never was a more faceless city or a more
deceptive one. It hasn't a face because it has too many,
all of them different – Patrick Nuttgens, 'Leeds: the
Back-to-Front, Inside-Out, Upside-Down City'.

. . . now blankness can speak through me in blank verse
of files official secrets thirty years,
all mention of their contents drawing blanks,
of one we blanked in life and dead, did not wake.
Our tale is paradoxographical,
since contradictions are what most defines
This squarèd circle of celestial bodies . . .
that's from Jonson's masque we're taking off
in memory of David Oluwale,
Saint David on the BNP blog
attacking what this theatre had planned.
He was a paradox, a Christian
and godson of Oceanus and Oshun
whose surname *Oluwale*'s Yoruba,
in English 'God Comes Home' – to God's Own County,
Yorkshire! what could be more right than that?
His last home was our Holy City centre,
final circle of his Christian hell,
a ring that boxed him in from Millgarth nick
to Armley Gaol and then the NHS
that locked him up a decade, did no good,
then turned him out again to homelessness
at Enoch Powell's 'Water Tower' speech,
And what you vowed was water,

And what you vowed was water . . .
though Jonson wrote that Africans don't dream,
Oluwale had a dream, followed it
then faded into it, a dream of Britain,
Britannia, whose new name makes all tongues sing . . .
In Ben's time *Britain* meant a tattered mask
repainted by its new and foreign king
to show how borders could just disappear
like dreams or plays, though now this mask's so snug
some wear it and pretend it is their face,
so they're not *E*NP, like *S*NP
but *B*NP, the xenophobes we chose
to stand for us in Europe's Parliament.
How upside-down, inside-out, back to front
yet right for this contrary God's own town.
Saint David, though I know you don't exist,
forgive me while I exit and get pissed.

Border Ballad

When Einstein built his box from thought
    to fix Uncertainty,
its non-existent clock inside
    unwound without a key;

it held no water either, Bohr
    was too polite to say,
while proving this thought experiment
    a dice that God would play.

The *'Flatland'* hero called 'A. Square'
    who'd think outside his box
gets taken on a pilgrimage
    beyond the orthodox.

In Pointland first to learn its views
    he went to see the King,
who couldn't see the point of him
    so wouldn't say a thing.

In Lineland next his *left*s and *right*s
    to locals seemed absurd;
where all is found with *up* and *down,*
    who needs another word?

In Spaceland, then back home he asked
    about the tesseract;
now everywhere agreed 'A. Square'
    was dangerously cracked.

They gaoled him so four solid walls
    would lend his own support;
they taught him intramurally
    to straighten out his thought.

This border ballad's walls first rose
    where Angle Land lacked order;
its laws were theoretical,
    debatable its border.

The pele tower of its verse contains
    a fear it will not hold,
that closed inside, none lived or died
    stayed young nor yet grew old;

more rooms than Hilbert's hotel boasts
    just make it more a Hell;
you'll hear no song nor dinner gong
    nor the horn of Gabriel,

as silent as the pele tower clock
    or its cat none ever saw
called Schrödinger, which does not purr
    but holds us in its paw;

no reason underlines its rules,
    no reason, only rhyme;
it needs no place, just ink, white space
    and what we think is time.

Darkness Visible

It is still remarkable how little attention is paid to Freemasonry in Wilde – John Schad, 'Queer Fish'

The exercising convicts tramped
   in silence round and round
as half-formed ballad verses rang
   the walls of Wilde's own mind;

but then a convict caught his eye,
   one of his Brotherhood,
who crossed both arms before his face,
   a Mason's sign of need.

Distressed by this experience
   Wilde saw the Governor,
who lent the grateful balladeer
   dark glasses he then wore

when walking round the Reading yard
   with his Masonic brother
to save him catching his sad eye
   for any further bother.

A paradox, Wilde could have said,
   illuminates the light,
while what the Craft illuminates
   I won't say, though I might.

Glass, Darkly

. . . but time lies bleeding: I too have to pass –
though on the subject of the double-take,
Pale Fire's false opening made my neck ache,
as must its bird's which hits the windowpane
it takes for how to get back out again;
but light reflected at its tunnel's end
was just another way this bird was penned
by John Shade's poem in the style of Pope
I'm putting underneath the microscope.
Since Irwin taught me how to up my grade
through shows of brilliance brilliantly displayed,
no bird brain I, I'm taking as my lamp
Shade's killer Jack, that 'transcendental tramp'
from Nova Zembla's fire and ice and frost
where art not realistic is art lost,
a wilderness of mirrors shelved like books
full of all faces but the one which looks.
A clockwork soldier, over land and ocean
Jack moves, we're told, in 'iambic motion'
on his *gradus ad Parnassum* west,
poeticidal, never needing rest,
a cardboard Commie from a comic book,
the ticking crocodile to Captain Hook
but painted post-war-paranoia red.
Though Senator McCarthy's namesake said
the book *Pale Fire* is a Jack-in-the-box
it's dozens, each a nested paradox,
(John Shade would use card boxes when he wrote
as did Nabokov: here, I made a note,
'Boxmaster' being a key Masonic job).

While 'Jack' suggests machine-part, card, Frost, yob,
then Jack Straw, *Jacquerie*, Jacques de Molay
whose Templars joined the Masons (Masons say),
this former glassworker's old surname, 'Gradus',
bends to 'D'Argus', soon to 'Leningradus',
but long before it turned into 'Degree',
I knew *Pale Fire* was shot with Masonry
from when Shade makes its 'G' his code for 'God',
while Mason socialists were far from odd
on Jack's dark European Continent.
Soon I'll prove all such references were meant
within the architecture of *Pale Fire*,
the Masons' spiral stair its final gyre –
a murdered architect's their founding myth!
I'm sure my thesis, here in gist and pith,
will get the good grade in my first degree,
that sets me up to take a Ph.D. . . .
excuse me: I do tend to ricochet
and 'Time is blood', as Chuikov would say
in Stalingradus. Getting up to speed,
we need to retrace where Jack's own steps lead:
'Hit the road, Jack' the song goes: so did Jack;
a Zemblan Shadow agent won't look back,
nor on a mission ever miss his home,
his purpose steady as a metronome –
though Mandelstam wrote 'limping like a clock',
now science says there's neither 'tick' nor 'tock',
but alternation human brains supplied
to time's torturing drips, like stillicide
on cowans' foreheads (*cowan*'s Masonry,
derived from 'dry stone waller' – OED),
those spies that Masons tie up under eaves.
Jack's god is Mercury, the god of thieves;

none take off faster from their starting blocks
(the proper wood for carving him is box),
but Jack is less a flier than a walker –
I seem to see in him Tarkovsky's *Stalker*,
whose expeditions through his Zemblan 'Zone'
in some ways seem reflections of Jack's own.
It's *Mirror* looks more John Shade's film to me,
what with Tarkovsky's father's poetry –
that 'like a fire without a shadow' line
alone's a seam I know I mean to mine,
then that shot where the bird breaks through the glass . . .

Whistling Or Just After . . .

. . . the Australian
It wasn't the blackbird, you write.
The blackbird's seen as it's seen at night,
as cute and fly as St Anselm's odd,
hovering, havering proof of God.

. . . the German
Hovering over/in the
poem, Celan's blackbird
on one wing but no prayer

. . . the North American
The SR-71 'Blackbird' stealth plane,
on an enemy's gridded round screen,
is so small in its Radar Cross Section,
it's never *was* but *might have been*.

. . . the Serbian
Kosovo, *'Blackbirds' Field'*,
dunged by believers' blood.
The silence of weapons
is a birdless silence.

. . . the English
the Muslim student being frisked
holds his arms outstretched
like Kevin practising crossfigill,
his palm a blackbird's nest.

. . . the Scots

The blackbird o'er the water,
a cuckoo in his nest:
fuck the pair o' 'em.

. . . the Irish

If you knew, as I do,
that blackbird's true story,
hard tears would blind you
to the High King of Glory.

. . . the Antrim Gaelic

The Rinn Seimhne blackbird hovers over home ground
watching Dummy Fluters play without making a sound;
muscle not musicians, they guard the band and mime,
on the look-out for fenians, they're trying to keep time.

. . . the Welsh

That dandy blackbird Death
all week wears Sunday best,
its eyes two golden rings:
sunrise and sunset.

. . . the Italian

The 'Inferno' cites January's 'Blackbird Days',
when at the first flash of New Year Sun
that proverbially stupid creature cries
God, I fear you no longer: Spring is come!

Now God is dead, this proverb forgotten,
every January's sunshine infernally longer
in our brave new world ruled by clever men,
the blackbird's song sounds brighter and stronger.

. . . the Spanish

One blackbird
in Paz's two gardens
but three minds.

. . . the French

Even when the blackbird walks,
we know that it has wings;
even when the poet talks,
we know she really sings.

. . . the Yiddish

When a translation
takes off like a blackbird,
or the song of a blackbird,
you have to worry.

Braque's Drum

Le tambour, instrument de la meditation. Qui ecoute le
tambour entend le silence – Braque

Georges Braque, 'e was an artist an' 'igh Cubist to the bone
   (Sir 'Enry Newbolt's spinnin' dahn below)
an' Stevens loved 'is Cubists an' 'e wasn't on 'is own,
   (an' spinnin' right beside 'im's Picasso)
so multiple perspective's are 'is *Blackbird*'s raison d'être
   (when such a view in art was comme il faut);
hence for this fractured eye on nature we're in Wally's debt
   (plus that poetry's another kind of dough).

But sometimes Stevens prized a sword as much as brush or pen
   (Sir 'Enry Newbolt's slowin' dahn below)
when writin' that the fighter is the master of all men,
   (now whirlin' like a turbine's ol' Pablo);
yet Braque implies the drum might teach us more without the fife
   (your split perspective takes in friend an' foe);
in war, the bloke 'oo talks like me is first to lose 'is life,
   (Tommy, Ivan, Fritz or G.I. Joe).

So I'll take Braque's drum to England an' I'll 'ang it on my wall,
   (ol' Newbolt's back to spinnin' dahn below)
an' I'll meditate on silence from the sofa where I'll sprawl
   (the grahnd is still on Pablo Picasso).
I'll 'ear the blackbird sing, then stop, an' keep on listenin' after,
   my love between 'em ditherin' to and fro,
an' look on Braque's square drum an' take a turn o' gentle laughter,
   (diminuendo, innuendo, go).

Alferi Stock

```
p  a  n  d  o  r  a  m  a
a  r  k  o  g  n  o  s  i
r  s  a  x  p  y  x  o  x
a  i  a  y  o  u  b  p  o
g  o  b  o  x  o  d  i  d
r  n  a  t  o  x  s  n  a
a  s  h  l  a  r  m  h  r
m  i  a  o  n  i  u  e  a
a  c  i  m  e  d  n  a  p
```

Heredity

Sterne detours into the future
to invent Debord's détournement,
recycling an attack on plagiarism
from 'The Anatomy of Melancholy':
. . . are we forever to be twisting
and untwisting the same rope?

My own sad anatomy recycles DNA,
the frayed rope of its double-helix
twists with optical fibre to slip past
all the Turnitin detection software
to a blank screen, *projecting trait*
and trace; passing on, passing off.

Jericho Shandy

The surrealist machine is more often than not
a nonfunctional machine – Sara Darius,
'The Senses of Modernism'

Returning from the anniversary
event for Sterne at Bradford Library,
a theft of signal wire maroons his train
beside the Kirkstall Abbey points for Leeds,
a name which sounds a pun, but not to him.
He's feeling hemmed-in by the open space,
a paradoxophobia mixed with . . .
he wonders what word would mean 'fear of nature' –
gaiaphobia? or start with 'pan-',
as in panic, as in panic attack?
He notes Cornell alarm chains under glass,
a hammer under glass for breaking glass.
This Bradford route's a sideline to a sideline,
sidelined now, reflecting on itself,
he thinks, a black-silk-hatted parody,
a *Soft Cell* synth man who only plays
recessionals on his harmonium
as doors close on the coffin and the flames.
He checks the carriage doors. They're locked, of course.
He notes the engine idles in iambics,
growing more insistent all the time.
Distraction from distraction's what he needs;
he thinks of Henry 'Box' Brown, escaped slave,
who recreated on this line his flight
to Northern freedom from Virginia,
and then of Earnshaw, the unescaped artist,

boxmaker, anarchist, who rode here
on his famed Surrealist Expeditions,
now travelling just as fast, although he's dead,
as this steel coffin with an Abbey view.
There's no one in his carriage. Or the next,
bar one slumped goth, a daywalker in shades.
He sees the guard is smoking down the track.
Reminded of that traveller's tale from Twain
with mummies fuelling Egyptian trains,
he opens all the carriage windows wide
then gets a head of steam up for himself.
The flesh is grass that fuels his Proto Pipe,
distraction engine of the connoisseur;
a locomotive run on loco weed,
but pocket-sized, its firebox solid brass
with built-in poker, tar-trap, sliding smoke-cap –
Ceci n'est pas une pipe, but art to him
from stem to Sternesque incurled spinning smoke
that rhymes with wire abandoned by the thieves
to kink and bite its tail and arabesque
like drawings of Trim's gestures with his stick.
He draws until his head begins to spin,
thinks Northern Lights a good name for this grass . . .
When straight, he'd kill time on another line
by taking phone cold-callers for a ride;
A timeshare? Great! But let's consider time!
He'd fugue on monastery prayer-routines
and Mumford's view their strictness gave the West
its grounding in machine-age discipline,
or Mrs Shandy winding up her husband;
Marx on clockless works; Toussaint L'Ouverture,
his gold watch stolen, exiled in the Jura,
where, in good time, the local watchmakers

would teach Kropotkin real-life anarchism . . .
None laughed, their English often second-hand,
commission making up their sweatshop pay,
his bourgeois deviationism stale,
reduced as one of Bennett's Talking Heads.
But now he listens with intensity
to sounds a swift makes harvesting the sky,
worms churning willowherb and meadowsweet,
the bull chained by its nose to a cartwheel,
a punky sun turning its wooden dial . . .
A tyre's soft watch drips slowly on a tree;
inside, paranoia's less critical
than *tumultuosissimamente*:
he's sure he's suffering Karmic punishment
for keeping hands from working in real life,
his Chinese watch, where copper scrap winds up,
the Golden Virginia in all those joints . . .
The robot heartbeat of the engine turns
to footsteps at his back, death in high heels,
while Kirkstall Abbey melts to Auden's face:
Stop all the clocks, cut off the telephone,
it says to Alan Bennett, *Poetry?*
But that's found far from outskirts such as these!
Remembering that Bennett lived near Troy,
by Horsforth Station, he thinks of Irwin,
Hector's foe, who lives there in the screenplay
though *Somewhere on the outskirts* on the stage;
then Bennett quoting Eliot on walls;
the History Boys against the National wall
on the book cover Darren Wall designed . . .
Convinced he's trapped now for eternity,
he thinks this page's walls are closing in,
then closes his own eyes to find himself

in his personal page 73:
he dreams evolved new fish will one day find
his cage of bones in the train's rusted cage
with Northern Lights' seeds growing through his ribs
a post-historic forest coast to coast,
his Proto Pipe all protozoic slime . . .
He shudders, then forgets why, at what.
He wonders if the goth brought chocolate.

A Room With A View

I don't know how any civilized person can watch TV,
let alone own a set – W. H. Auden

But now I see civilization through new square eyes
since buying a TV with two square metres of screen.
Better than Debord at seeing through the spectacle
to the bone beneath the bling, it focusses as fairly
on the diva's bleached moustache as choral acne,
with equal liquid-crystal clarity from gods to stalls.
Brilliant as walls of Pre-Raphaelites, TV is wallpaper
beyond Morris, more human because it is moving,
which can inspire us all to poetry as it did Ashbery,
like the campfires our half-ape ancestors watched,
evolving so they'd be able to change the channel.

Night Cube

With one show over, the gallery-goers gone,
in the darkness, it is the empty white room
takes centre stage in strobes of headlights
from passing traffic, reeling off its whole set
in flickering tableaux as if stills from old films:
Jeff Wall lightbox; Joseph Cornell shadow box;
Borg ambulance; Zen dice; God's television;
perfected Masonic ashlar; the Ka'aba Stone,
before darkened by the sinful breath of men;
now a silver negative of the New Jerusalem
in its heavenly flight, fugitive as this poem
melting on its page like a cube of black ice.

A Gift of Boxes

for Michael Longley

Under Kublai's dragon fan, a hexagram's unbroken lines
suggest Yuan as the name for his new Mongol dynasty,
a nomad staking his future on a game of Chinese boxes.
His palace is a square city in the square city of Xanadu.

Square ripples on a soldier's hem in Giotto's *Arena* cycle
suggest to some scholars the new Yuan 'square script',
(*for writing all languages under Heaven*) or a pastiche,
based on the artist's glimpses inside a merchant's ledger.

In Xamdu did Cublai Can . . . ripples of Purchas' words
wash up in an opium warrior's poetry and broken lines,
his imperial torpor broken by a Marco Polo from Porlock,
a distraction from his pen, setting his mind to wander.

II

In one of my metempsychotic episodes, suddenly
I remember I am Jesuit missionary Matteo Ricci
bringing Pythagorean wonders to the Ming court.

I build memory theatres in the heads of its scholars –
not just their civil service examination candidates –
hoping some find room for the drama of the Mass.

I painted the Emperor's portrait by our new art,
explaining to him the perspective-box it came in,
its lines flowing to one point like roads to Rome.

He had me Chinese the Greeks, fix clocks, maps,
compose a cycle of lyrics for his eunuch choir,
accompany them on my gift of a harpsichord –

If you move away can you leave yourself behind?
this was a line about moving I meant to be moving.
It moved both the Emperor and eunuchs to laughter.

III

Another of my funerals will detour by the Clock Tower
at Shipley, a modernist white cube which lords it over
Market Square, like the Puck goat at Killorglin's Fair.
Though known to coarse locals as Picasso's Bollock,
lovers meet under it, who will ignore our digression
peeling off for the Terra Ovidiana of Brimham Rocks,
where even stones lose their hardness and rigidity.
Cross-bedded feldspar, gritstone, quartz are tricks
of northern light, kaleidoscopes which might spill us
anywhere but to rhyme with Shipley, choose Ripley.
By its 'Hotel de Ville', they'll post my coffin for duty
in the wobbly sentry-box inscribed '*Parlez au Suisse*',
to guard the road to a castle rebuilt as 'Das Schloss'.
This village is not just Yorkshire but most of Europe:
any smaller, it would have room enough for universes
with more inside them, each one larger than its host,
a Ptolomaic nest as made by Guard MacCruiskeen.

IV

The way your poetry stacks up now, Michael,
makes another gift of magic boxes,

squaring the circle of words and music,
a feathered nest where eggs already sing

in languages for imaginary birds;
their wings fan open like pages of a book –

I see more in your poems all the time,
and more fans everywhere each time I look.

Death Panels

1 Hildegardmedezin

'You jaundiced should stun a bat
then strap it to your loins to die.
Capercaillie-bladder clears maggots
as pulverized turbot-liver does wall-eye.

Bake epileptics a cake of mole's blood,
duck-beaks and goose-feet with spelt.
A broth of hamsters relieves scrofula
while sparrowhawk-butter cools lust.

Mad dogs fed on lark-heads will recover;
if not, powder their tongues for ulcers
or cobble a pair of shoes from their skin
to ease bunions or persistent blisters . . . '

2 Resurrectionists

Burke's the butcher, Hare the thief,
Knox the boy who buys the beef;
a Scottish children's skipping rhyme
with killing ways for killing time.

The Law absolved Hare of all sin
who sold his friend to save his skin
while Burke's skin bound a trophy book
in Edinburgh: go take a look;

you needn't read between its lines
for Draculas or Frankensteins,
for Knox as Jekyll, Burke his Hyde
whose own hide paid for those who died –

to put these horrors in their place,
see Dr Knox's book on race
where *race is all*, its author felt.
The worst he lists? *The Irish Celt*.

Burke the butcher, Hare the thief,
Knox the boy who bought their beef:
Burke sold corpses, Hare the quick,
Knox the doctor made us sick.

The Origin of Pestilence

Kalevala VL

Loviatar, worst daughter of Death,
half-blind virgin, darker with pain,
with the mother of all pain: birth:

she curses, cold clawing her bones,
in the road, her first childbed; curses
her womb's ninemoonsworth of strife.

Her tears steam and hiss; teeth crack;
she flies up to a gap between crags
to hang for help from gravity's drag,

back down for hot springs; into snow,
then a cataracts' back-breaking force;
none any help. Sky rings with her din.

At last God orders this grievous girl
to North Farm, its hag to midwife her,
freeing her foetus for mischief abroad.

There, in a hovel encircled by bogs,
to birthing charms droned by a witch
Loviatar opens, drops us her dread load.

A Summer's Fancy

for Peter Didsbury

One day, soon after I died, I returned to Hull,
for my sins, on a literary pilgrimage, in honour
of a poet who publishes his books back to front,
if not upside-down and inside-out. But passing
Menwith's Pox Americana, my GPS went AWOL;
soon I found myself genuflecting at the obelisk
to the Wold Newton Stone, found by the son
of Didius who quickened Sterne into literature.
For a meteor is a poem, a linguistic firework
declining between *meteoroid* and *meteorite*,
dreamt on as Cybele, Grail, Ark of Plague,
panspermic rain. This anti-philosopher's stone
shattered the glass houses which Aristotle built
on Eudox's foundations, then Ptolemy glazed;
a solar system of frozen ripples, discrete crystal
Chinese onionskins, sterile Russian doll-wombs
contraceiving intercourse between planets. *Those
who live in glass houses shouldn't write poems*,
as the Zemblan said to the poet, hopelessly lost:
*Ask where's the North? At York 'tis on the Tweed
On Tweed 'tis at the Orcades, and there
At Greenland, Zembla or the Lord knows where* . . .
When I finally penetrated the ring road to Hull,
a rosary of sausages, hungry for more miracles,
at a butcher's shop I prayed while its proprietor
bickered with some his customers about Arianism,
the consubstantiality of the Logos and His Father.
Distracted by their argument, I took a butcher's

at the shop window, where I suddenly perceived
that I'd fathered a reflection poxy with raindrops,
which careered down the glass and special offers
like Hippodrome chariots. Although a pluviophile
of the complex lodge, equipped with handshakes
if not the Butcher's Apron, I am nevertheless also
the Emperor Justinian in the worst year of my reign,
alone in my imperial box, occluded by rising dust
from horses' hooves, enduring Blues' and Greens'
Mexican waves, their theological abuse in verse
which stresses the penultimate or antepenultimate
syllables in each line. The Empire is a plague to me,
a flea-circus, and I miss my Empress Theodora,
who knew about circuses. There squats Procopius,
thinking I don't know about his filthy *Anekdota*.
Wanker. He makes me feel the need to scratch,
to frisk myself for buboes, or at least fleabites.
Rats are to thank for this, little feet skittering
across the Byzantine mosaic of this Greek poem,
millions in the record harvests of the century
flooding my narthex as the San Marco Basilica
will flood one day under our plundered horses,
or a Yorkshire street in what they call summer
with meteors of water, unbegotten, uncreated
rain, both pre-existing and superior to the sun.

Year of the Rat, Rat of the Year

At the N.F.R.S. Show
they're playing the Stranglers –
Rattus Norvegicus:
the Fancy's at Bradford.

The New Wave floods in,
now more goth than punk;
the mohicans wilt
on the no-longer-young.

I'm here for the poetry
bred in these shades,
the gradings of love,
the songs of its names:

Flame Point, Champagne,
Opal, Mink, Dove,
American Berkshire,
Agouti Buff,

Cinnamon Pearl,
Silver Fawn Rex,
Chocolate, Topaz
the Dark-Eyed Self.

My Grandfather's Seed-Fiddle

To guide him in his sowing, white rags are stuck
along may hedges on each side of the field;
as the scarecrow opens its arms to conduct,
he straps himself into his new seed-fiddle.

Like notes, the seed plays over his furrows
to the rhythm of his walk and his bowing;
he dreams of reaping even as he sows.
Tomorrow, birds will read his music, and sing.

Closed Inquiry

Santon Bridge's Annual Lying Championship,
being an amateur event, bars all politicians.
Prizes are hogged by agricultural braggadocio
in the style of Airedale Heifers or Skipton Tups:

cattle so huge they need individual postcodes,
rams' horns winding up in different time-zones,
pigs warping Earth's magnetic field and so on.
Later, the contest over, all the visitors gone,

they talk of *dead holes*, often doing so by not,
representing them by gaps in the conversation,
their mention a breach, their existence a breach,
avoiding new charges for the disposal of bodies.

But in lambing season, roadkill of badgers drawn
by smells out of their knowledge suggests them.
Questioning spades could turn up for the books
corpses, fur-edged like old pages, rank and filed.

The Grassington Mandala

The photograph, a monk explains,
shows statues once in Bamiyan;
near here the Pilgrimage of Grace
fought Bluff King Henry's Taliban,

where this enlightened refugee
rebuilds the Buddha's house in sand –
though formerly crushed precious stones,
he laughs, now any dust's as sound.

The sun and moon attend his throne
surrounded by five jewelled walls;
a foursquare palace circles both
(with, on its roof, white parasols),

then rosaries of thunderbolts,
and rainbow-serpent aureoles;
each high brocaded gate supports
two kneeling deer with dharma wheels.

This Mitrukpa Mandala's power,
to these who travel with belief,
absolves the karma of who kill
or are involved in taking life.

The RAF train overhead –
Jihadists also, up the Dale;
a homeless monk with steady hands:
another serpent bites its tail.

False Friends

I am the son of the highway . . . all languages,
all prayers belong to me – Maalouf, 'Leo l'Africain'

I'd rather be insulted in Arabic than praised
in other tongues, we say. Insulted in Arabic
due to my Christian translators – *traduttore*
traditore. Still, I'm known. Poets aren't proud.

One hadith damns all authors using 'I' for pride,
but my own *I*s make up a pride: Leo l'Africain
Leo Africanus, Giovanni Leone, Yuhann al-Asad,
Born al-Wazza, 'the Weigher' now weighs words:

barbarian's root barb with our *Barbara*, 'Berber',
from 'babble'; your *stanza*, 'verse' but also 'room'
with our *bait*, 'verse' and 'tent'. Places poets live.
The Arabic language has been less faithful than I:

maskara's bastards? 'The Masque of Blackness',
where I take a bow; make up I wear for Yeats;
named for the pope I was given to as a slave,
my mask of whiteness. Still, at least I'm known.

Hollow Man

Writers' blocks are philosopher's stones
that turn words into golden silence,
but Martin Bell proved his wizardry
by turning his own block into poetry.

One round hole he couldn't square;
a peg stuck fast, reduced to write,
'Leeds is Hell nor am I out of it!'
while mostly out of it everywhere.

The Party was once his life and soul,
but then he read *Darkness at Noon*.
Other lights failed him, one by one,
till it was dark all day for Martin Bell.

I'd watch him in our local drinking,
a would-be sorcerer's apprentice
who'd read him, meant to thank him
but I said nothing. Gutless. Jealous.

Rombald's Moor

One giant grabbed words
frozen in the northern air
which thawed, chattering
ouououon, goth, magoth . . .

his brother magoth froze
in this thunderous name,
his shallow grave; its bogs,
his rotting flesh; his bones,

outcropping millstone grit;
dark clouds, his brooding
over Lilliput Ilkley, looking
up agog, thunderstruck.

Lying Over the Ground

The song was supposed to lie over the ground in an
unbroken chain of couplets – Bruce Chatwin, 'Songlines'

Unbroken couplets chain my nightmares still
since reading this on some antique shop bill;
Hide your diminished heads, nor vainly talk
Among friends of how rapidly you walk:
First in the Annals of Pedestrian Fame
Historians will enter Bob Russell's name!
Too quickly through my sleep rings dead Bob's boast,
while in the blistering slipstream of his ghost,
I dream he's taking Nerval for a drag,
his lobster flying behind them like a flag,
as down the gasping boulevards they race!
Distracted rambling's more the poet's pace.
Some Aboriginals Bruce Chatwin met
will say to learn the way their mind had set
requires more openness than Chatwin showed
as he careered along their open road
through Alice Springs, as through a looking-glass.
Like time, Bruce Chatwin only came to pass
through Australia into his private Oz –
although we shouldn't be surprised, because
your traveller's tales were always fairy tales,
since publishers don't want a poet's sales
but books 'with legs' that run out of the shop,
not those that stroll, then stop, then stroll, then stop;
returns are part of going for a song,
which takes so long because it takes so long.
To poets and their readers, words are grace;

their roads best taken at an easy pace,
while even better than an easy pace is
entropy, collapse, then total stasis –
lots of poets write their best in bed:
the truly great among them are all dead.

Notes

Boxeur Nègre The great Nigerian boxer Dick Tiger had championship-winning careers at home, in Britain and then the U.S.A. After his retirement from boxing, he worked as a guard at the Metropolitan Museum of Art in New York.

'Strata' Smith William Smith earned the nickname as a result of his 1815 geological map, which revolutionised the science.

Unmaking This was written to accompany a proposed essay by Kester Aspden to be called 'The Unmaking of the English Working Class'.

Jericho Shanty Inspired by Philippa Troutman's travelling exhibition 'The Shanties of Ribblehead'. For this series of etchings, she researched the work-camps of the viaduct's builders, one of which was the Jericho Shanty. The *OED* defines 'Jericho', among other things, as 'Used in slang or colloquial phrases for . . . a place far distant and out of the way', while *Brewer's* glosses the phrase 'Go to Jericho' as 'Go and hang yourself', 'Go to hell', and 'I wish you were at Jericho' as 'Anywhere out of my way'. 'Foul bite' occurs when the ground breaks down on a plate being etched, allowing the acid to spread into unwanted areas. 'Left-footer', like someone 'who digs with the left foot', means a Catholic, presumably to evoke 'sinister' associations, although right-handed people will naturally dig with the left foot. The last section of this poem is made withfragments from Michael Alexander's translation of thefragmentary Anglo-Saxon poem 'The Ruin'.

Via Negativa The ending quotes a Leeds United supporters' chant.

from **'The Masque of Blankness'**   The presentation this is taken from was performed at West Yorkshire Playhouse, directly opposite Millgarth Police Station. Officers based here were involved in the systematic abuse of David Oluwale, who drowned in the river Aire having been chased there by policemen. Occam's Razor notwithstanding, alternative theories concerning Oluwale's killers still circulate, including on the internet in 2009 that he was a victim of Masonic assassins. 'The Holy City' is an old anti-Semitic nickname for Leeds.

Death Panels   P. D. Curtin describes Knox, Burke and Hare's principal customer, on the basis of his later writings, as 'the real founder of British racism'.

Year of the Rat, Rat of the Year   N.F.R.S. stands for National Fancy Rat Society.

Closed Inquiry   My informant on farming matters to do with 'dead holes' (there will be other regional expressions for these illegal burials) wishes to remain anonymous.

The Grassington Mandala   The last verse refers to the fact that Jihadists such as the 7/7 bombers trained, among other places, in the Yorkshire Dales.

False Friends   Poet, translator, historian and travel writer among many other things, 'Leo Africanus' was also one of W. B. Yeats' spirit guides.

Acknowledgements

A number of these poems have already appeared elsewhere, and acknowledgements are therefore due to the editors of *Poetry London*, *Poetry Review*, *Poetry Ireland Review*, the *Guardian*, *Yorkshire Evening Post*, *Stand*, *Northern Lights*, *Real Fits*, *Qualm*, *Spine*, *Moving Worlds*, *New Writing 13* and the *Warwick Review*. A version of 'Via Negativa' appeared in *The Hounding of David Oluwale* by Kester Aspden (Vintage, 2008). 'Night Cube' was commissioned by *Art World* magazine for Issue 3 (February 2008) with a feature on the cube in art. '*from* "the Masque of Blankness"' originally formed part of *God Comes Home*, a dramatic piece presented at West Yorkshire Playhouse in February 2008. 'A Gift of Boxes' was written for Michael Longley's seventieth-birthday festschrift *Love Poet, Carpenter* published by Enitharmon in July 2009. 'Róisín Bán' appeared in the *Contourlines* anthology edited by Neil Wenborn and M. E. J. Hughes (Salt, 2009). 'Beggar's Song' and sections of other poems here first appeared as text for the composer Christopher Fox's 'Natural Science', premiered at the Soundwaves festival in Brighton, July 2010, by Trio Scordatura. I am grateful to Gail Earnshaw for her permission to use as the cover of this book an image derived from her late husband Tony Earnshaw's box 'The Blind Engine Driver'. For the name 'Pandorama', I am principally indebted to Bert White's contraption in Robert Tressell's *The Ragged Trousered Philanthropists*. Finally, I would like to record my thanks to the Arts Council, Yorkshire, for a grant which enabled me to finish this book.